Snowflakes

CREATIVE PAPER CUTOUTS
FOR ALL SEASONS

CINDY HIGHAM

GIBBS SMITH
TO ENRICH AND INSPIRE HUMANKIND

First Edition
23 22 21 20 19   5 4 3 2 1

Text and illustrations © 2019 Cindy Higham

Published by
Gibbs Smith
P.O. Box 667
Layton, Utah 84041

1.800.835.4993 orders
www.gibbs-smith.com

Cover design by Jess Cruickshank
Printed and bound in China

Gibbs Smith books are printed on either recycled, 100% post-consumer waste, FSC-certified papers or on paper produced from sustainable PEFC-certified forest/controlled wood source. Learn more at www.pefc.org.

Library of Congress Control Number: 2018967541

ISBN: 978-1-4236-5244-1

Contents

Getting Started

It's been said that no two snowflakes are alike. That's also true with paper snowflakes! Everyone in the family can cut out the same pattern and they will all look a little different. The slightest change in the paper folding or the smallest cut difference will give you a new and entirely unique snowflake.

Use this book as a tool to learn the techniques, and then start experimenting on your own. This book has some very simple patterns along with some that are more difficult. There is something for everyone! The pattern you are to cut out is shown in the wedge shape on the bottom of each page. Your job is to cut out the white part of the pattern. As you're flipping through the book, look at each pattern (not the entire snowflake) in order to determine how easy or difficult the snowflake will be to create.

How to Use the Patterns in This Book

Trace or photocopy the pattern you want to use. Each pattern is made for 8 $^1/_2$ x 11-inch paper. Set the pattern aside.

Select a paper that is not too thick—standard copy paper works well. Anything very heavy will be difficult to cut through. The sharper your scissors are, the easier it is to cut the snowflakes, and the better they will turn out. You won't need to use the point on the end of the scissor blade, so blunt-end scissors are great for children.

Use the folding instructions on page 8 to learn how to fold your paper. Fold the paper with the edges tucked in tight to get the best snowflake. You should now have a folded paper triangle.

Pick up your snowflake pattern and tape it to your folded paper triangle. The best way to do this is to put a small piece of tape on each side of the pattern, and then fold the tape over onto the paper triangle.

Cut out the white part of the pattern. Cut the small sections first, and then work your way up to the larger cuts. This will give you more paper to hold onto for a longer amount of time.

After you have finished cutting, remove the tape and carefully unfold the snowflake.

Press out the folds in the paper by folding the creases backward so they flatten out. You can also press the snowflake with a warm iron, or you can lay it flat in a book for a day or two.

Decorating Your Snowflakes

If you want to make your snowflakes sparkle, you can use glue sticks with glitter in them or glue glitter pens. Use colored paper to give your snowflakes variety. You can also try different types of paper, or even shiny foil or wrapping paper. (When using paper with a design on it, fold your paper so the printed side is on the inside. That way the tape won't pull the design off the paper.) Children will love to use crayons, colored pencils, or markers to decorate their snowflakes.

The finished snowflakes are perfect for scrapbooking, holiday cards, and decorating.

You can also use your snowflake patterns as quilt blocks, stencils, crochet patterns, wood ornaments, or patterns for stained glass!

Folding Instructions

If your paper is a rectangle, fold the top right corner down to the left side of the paper so that the top edge aligns with the left edge. Cut off the paper that extends past the bottom of the triangle. Unfold the paper, and now you have a square.

Diagram 1

Fold corner A down to B. (After each fold, run your fingernail along the fold to press it down tight.)

Fold corner C down to D. You should have a triangle that looks like the shaded area on the diagram.

Diagram 2

Fold the triangle as illustrated. Fold A to A, B to B, and C to C.

Diagram 3

Now fold in the opposite side. Fold A to A, B to B, and C to C. Make sure the folds are tight. The more precisely the paper is folded, the more precise the snowflake will be.

Diagram 4

Your paper should now look like this. On one side of the folded paper you will see a straight line, where the dotted line is shown in the diagram. Cut off the paper along this line. You now have your snowflake triangle and are ready to choose a pattern to make.

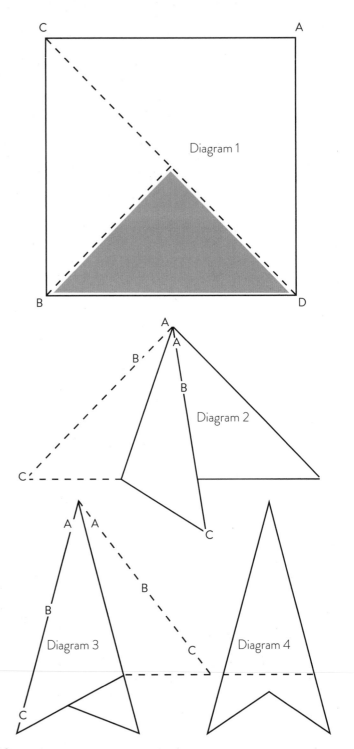

8

New Year's Hour Glass

13

Hearts with Arrows

15

Burst of Hearts

Hearts and Diamonds

Chandelier

Shamrocks

Carnations

Tulip Garden

Flying Kites

Lilies and Baby Chicks

41

Seashells

43

Shooting Stars

47

Statue of Liberty

49

Autumn Leaves

Big Bats

Spiderweb, Thick

Spider Legs

Claws and Pincers

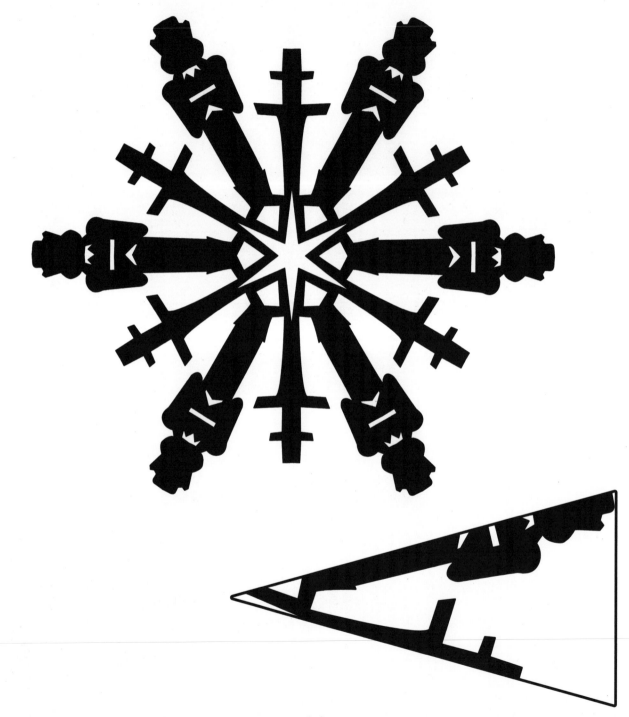

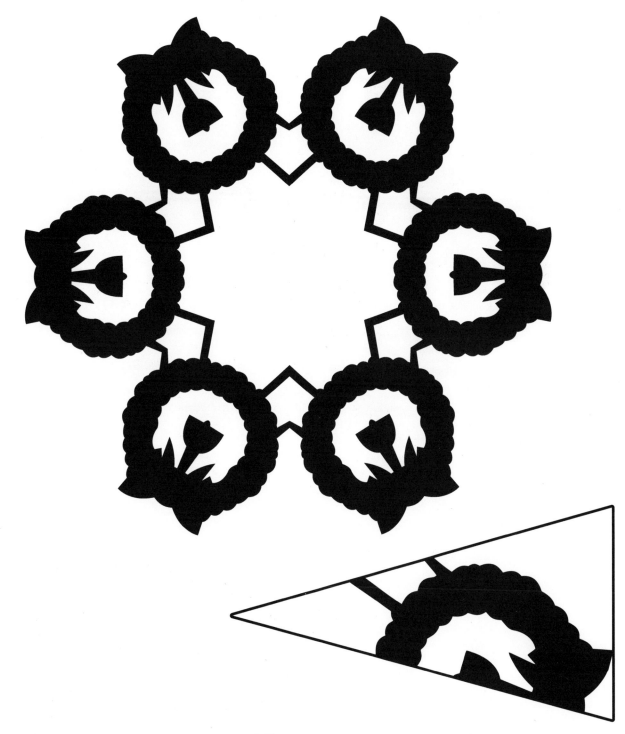

Mistletoe

Ballet

Christmas Tree Ornaments

Pine Grove

Candlelight

Star Over Bethlehem

Christmas Cookies

Ice Crystals

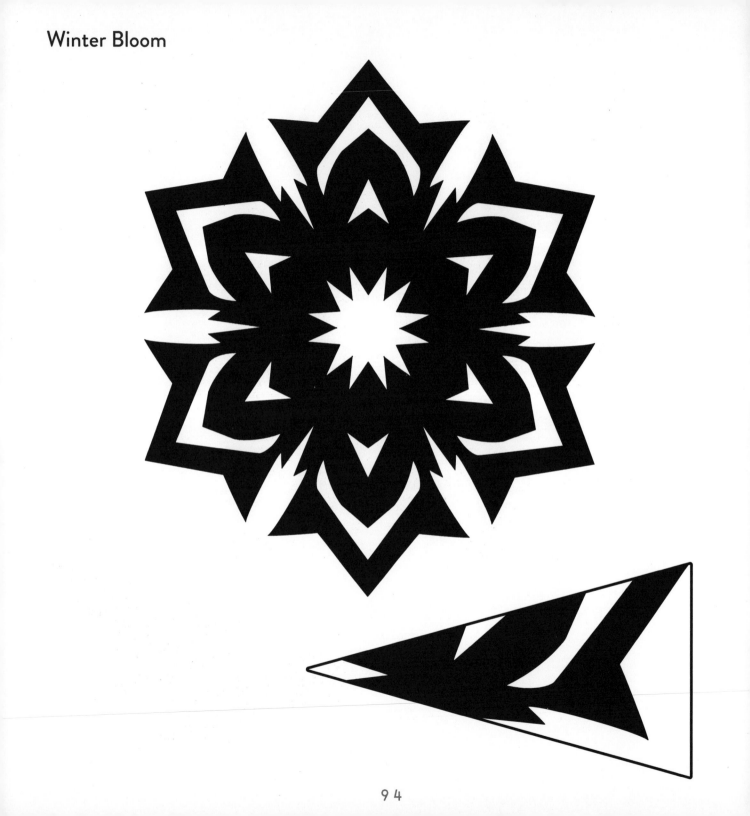

98

Pine Cone

Snowflake Hearts

Thistle

Pine Bough

Arrowheads

Tree House

Spaceship

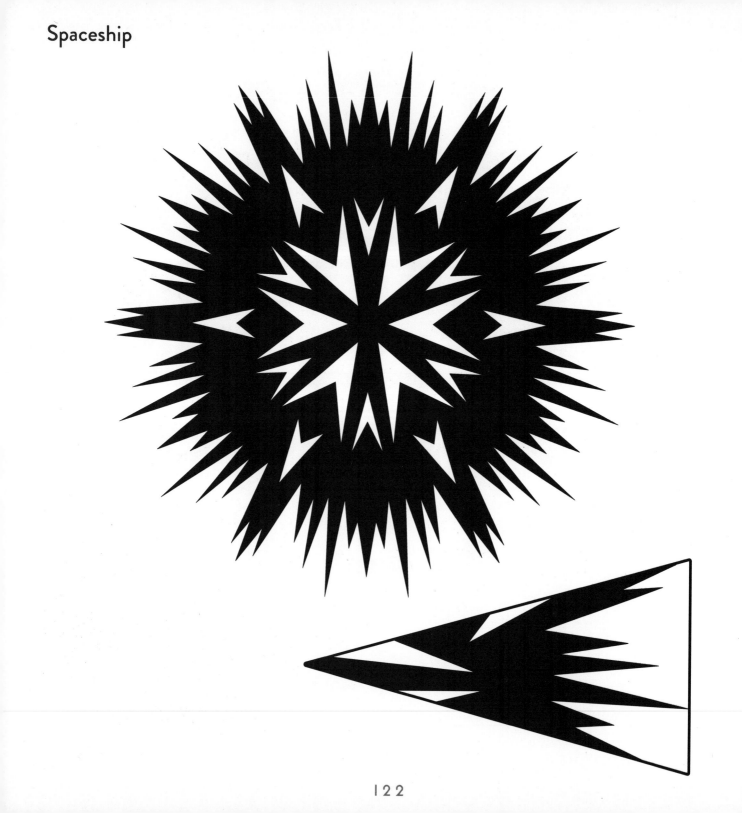

Dog

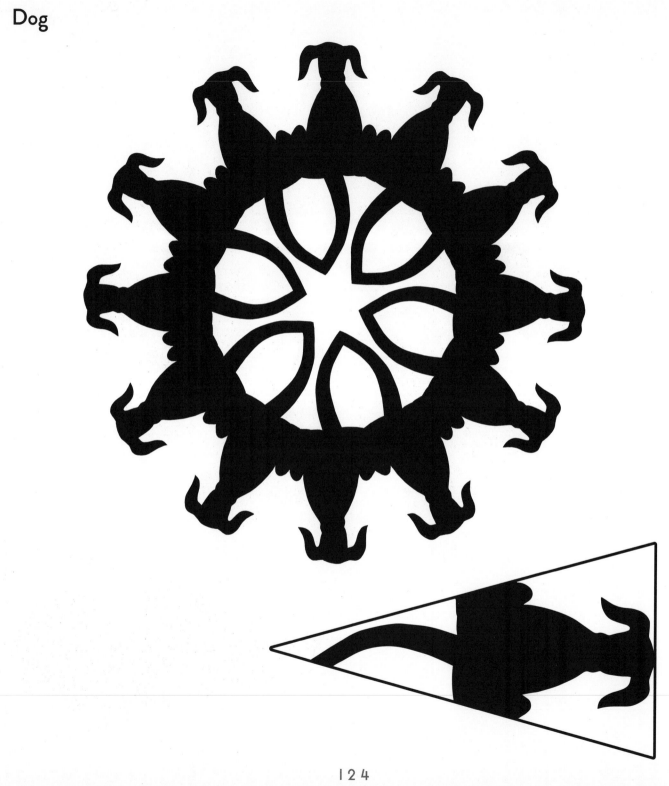

125

Venus Flytrap

Jets in Formation

Football

Fleur-de-Lis

143

Cactus Grove

Windmill

Doily

Kaleidoscope